Kung Fu Mind Training: Zero-Second Survival Instincts Manual

Rewire Your Brain for Instant Threat Response Using Ancient Martial Arts Psychology

By

Liang Wei Hao

Copyright © 2025 by Liang Wei Hao

All rights reserved. No part of this publication may be reproduced, stored in a retrieval system, or transmitted in any form or by any means, electronic, mechanical, photocopying, recording, or otherwise, without the prior written permission of the copyright owner, except for brief quotations in critical reviews or articles.

Prologue

This book teaches how to rewire your brain and body for instant reactions in dangerous situations. It combines ancient martial arts wisdom with practical modern training methods to help you develop automatic survival instincts. You'll learn how to move faster than thought, control fear, and respond effectively under extreme stress.

The training focuses on simple, repeatable techniques that work when adrenaline is high and fine motor control is low. It shows how to build reliable reflexes through specific drills that program your nervous system for real-world threats. The methods come from centuries of proven combat experience, not theory or sport fighting.

Breath control, mental focus, and body awareness form the foundation of this system. You'll discover how to stay calm when others panic, see threats before they develop, and act decisively without hesitation. The book explains why traditional martial artists spent years practicing basic movements and how to apply those principles to modern self-defense.

Physical skills are only part of the training. Equal attention goes to developing the warrior mindset - the unshakable mental toughness that keeps you fighting when others would quit. You'll learn how ancient fighters trained their minds to handle pain, fatigue, and uncertainty without breaking focus.

The techniques work for anyone regardless of age or fitness level. They rely on natural body mechanics rather than strength or flexibility. Police, military personnel, and security experts use similar methods to prepare for life-or-death situations where hesitation means disaster.

This isn't about becoming a fighter - it's about gaining the confidence that comes from knowing you can protect yourself. The training takes just minutes a day but creates lasting changes in how your brain and body respond to danger. Whether you want practical self-defense skills or simply greater peace of mind, these methods deliver real results.

TABLE OF CONTENTS

Prologue 3
TABLE OF CONTENTS 8
Chapter 1 10
The Warrior's Mindset 10
Chapter 2 17
Breathing Like a Fighter 17
Chapter 3 27
Seeing Danger Before It Comes 27
Chapter 4 38
No Thoughts, Just Action 38
Chapter 5 49
Fear Is Your Friend 49
Chapter 6 62
The Body Remembers 62
Chapter 7 79
The Invisible Shield 79
Chapter 8 94
One Move, One Kill 94
Chapter 9 108
Stress Training 108
Chapter 10 126
The Unbreakable Mind 126
About the Author 143

Chapter 1
The Warrior's Mindset

The first thing you need to understand is that your mind is your strongest weapon–stronger than your fists, stronger than any tool or weapon you might carry. A warrior isn't just someone who fights; a warrior is someone who *thinks* differently. Most people panic when danger comes. Their brains freeze, their bodies lock up, and they lose precious seconds trying to figure out what to do. But in real survival situations, you don't have seconds. You have zero seconds. That's why the warrior mindset isn't about being fearless–it's about training your mind to act *before* fear can stop you. Think of it like this: if someone throws a punch at your face, you don't have time to decide whether to block or dodge. Your body just does it. That's instinct. And instinct isn't magic–it's training.

So how do you build this mindset? It starts with understanding that fear is normal, but hesitation is deadly. Ancient martial artists didn't train just to fight–they trained to *survive*. They knew that in battle, thinking too much gets you killed. That's why they drilled their movements over and over until they didn't have to think anymore. They trusted their bodies to react before their brains could mess things up. You need to do the same. The modern world has made us soft. We overthink everything. We wait for permission to act. We second-guess ourselves. But in a real fight–or any life-or-death situation–there's no time for that. You have to rewire your brain to move first and think later.

This doesn't mean you act recklessly. It means you train so deeply that the right move comes out automatically. Imagine walking–you don't think about every step, do you? Your body just does it. Now imagine if fighting or escaping danger was that natural. That's the goal. To get there, you have to practice until your reactions are faster than your thoughts. Start small. When you hear a loud noise, don't jump–*observe*. Train yourself to stay calm and scan for threats instead of panicking. When something unexpected happens, pause for half a second–but *only* half a second–then act. That tiny pause keeps you from reacting blindly, but it's short enough that you don't freeze.

Another key part of the warrior mindset is *accepting* danger instead of pretending it doesn't exist. Most people live in denial. They think, "Bad things won't happen to me." But warriors know better. They expect danger. They prepare for it. That doesn't mean they're paranoid–it means they're ready. When you accept that threats are real, you stop being surprised by them. And when you're not surprised, you react faster. Think of it like driving a car. If you're alert, you can brake in time if someone cuts you off. But if you're daydreaming, you'll crash. Life is the same way. Stay sharp.

Finally, the warrior mindset is about *control*–not just control over your body, but control over your emotions. Anger, fear, panic–these will get you killed if you let them take over. But if you master them, they become fuel. Fear keeps you alert. Anger gives you power. The trick is to use them without letting them use *you*. Next time you feel afraid, don't try to push it away. Feel it, then channel it. Turn it into speed. Turn it into focus. That's how warriors turn weakness into strength.

This is just the beginning. The warrior mindset isn't something you learn in a day. It's a habit–a way of life. The more you practice, the stronger it gets. And the stronger it gets, the faster you'll react when it matters. No hesitation. No doubt. Just action. That's the difference between surviving and losing. That's the warrior way.

Chapter 2
Breathing Like a Fighter

Breathing is something we do without thinking, but the way you breathe can mean the difference between staying calm under pressure or losing control when it matters most. Fighters and martial artists have known this for thousands of years– the right kind of breath keeps you sharp, steady, and ready to move in an instant. If you've ever been so scared that your chest tightened and your breath came in short gasps, you know how quickly fear can take over. But if you train your breathing the right way, you can stop panic before it starts. This isn't about complicated techniques or mystical practices. It's about simple, proven methods that keep your mind clear and your body relaxed, even in the middle of chaos.

One of the oldest methods is slow, deep breathing from the belly, not the chest. When you breathe shallowly, your body thinks something is wrong, and that triggers stress. But deep, controlled breaths tell your brain that everything is okay, even when it's not. Try this: put one hand on your chest and the other on your stomach. Breathe in slowly through your nose, letting your stomach rise while your chest stays still. Hold it for a second, then let it out through your mouth, pushing out all the air. Do this five times, and you'll feel the difference immediately. Your heart rate slows, your muscles loosen, and your mind gets clearer. This works because it activates the part of your nervous system that calms you down, the opposite of the fight-or-flight response.

Another key trick is timing your breath to your movements. In martial arts, fighters exhale sharply when they strike or block. This isn't just for show–it tightens the core, adds power to the movement, and keeps you from holding your breath in tense moments. If you've ever lifted something heavy and grunted without thinking, you've done this naturally. The same idea applies in a fight or any high-pressure situation. When you react to danger, your breath should match your action—short, forceful exhales for quick moves, long steady breaths when you need to stay still and focused. If you practice this enough, it becomes automatic, and that means you stay in control instead of gasping for air when adrenaline hits.

Adrenaline is another reason breathing matters so much. When something scary happens, your body floods with adrenaline—your heart races, your muscles tense, and your senses sharpen. This is good if you need to run or fight, but only if you don't let it overwhelm you. Most people either freeze or panic because they don't know how to handle the rush. But if you train your breathing, you can ride that wave instead of drowning in it. One way to practice is by putting yourself under mild stress–like holding your breath for short bursts or doing quick sprints–then forcing yourself to breathe slowly right after. This teaches your body to recover fast and stay cool under pressure. Over time, you'll learn to stay calm even when your heart is pounding.

There's also something called "combat breathing," used by soldiers and martial artists to stay focused in life-or-death situations. It's simple: breathe in for four seconds, hold for four, breathe out for four, hold for four, and repeat. This rhythm keeps your mind from racing and stops panic before it starts. It works because counting gives your brain something to focus on besides fear, and the steady pace keeps your body balanced. You can use this anytime—before a confrontation, during a stressful moment, or even just to clear your head when things feel overwhelming. The more you practice, the faster you can drop into this calm state, no matter what's happening around you.

The connection between breath and emotion is something people have understood for centuries. In ancient China, warriors used breathing exercises to build endurance and mental strength. In Japan, samurai practiced controlled breathing to stay calm before battle. Even today, special forces soldiers and elite athletes use these same principles to perform under extreme pressure. The science backs it up–studies show that controlled breathing lowers stress hormones, improves focus, and even boosts physical performance. It's not magic; it's just how the body works. When you control your breath, you control your mind, and when you control your mind, you control the situation.

The best part is that you don't need any special equipment or training to start. You can practice anywhere-sitting at your desk, standing in line, or lying in bed. The key is consistency. Spend just a few minutes a day working on your breathing, and over time, it will become second nature. Then, when something stressful happens, your body will already know what to do. You won't have to think about staying calm–you'll just *be* calm. And in a real fight or emergency, that split-second advantage can save your life.

Breathing might seem too simple to make a difference, but that's exactly why it works. In the middle of chaos, the most basic things–like steady air moving in and out of your lungs–can keep you grounded. It's not about fancy techniques or secret knowledge. It's about training something you already do every day so that when the moment comes, your body doesn't fail you. That's what fighters have known for centuries, and that's what you can use to sharpen your instincts, right here, right now. Start today. Breathe deep, stay calm, and move when it's time to move. The rest will follow.

Chapter 3
Seeing Danger Before It Comes

The ability to spot trouble before it reaches you is what separates those who survive from those who get caught off guard. This isn't about being paranoid or seeing threats where there aren't any - it's about training your eyes and mind to notice the small details that most people miss. Think about how animals in the wild survive. They don't wait until the predator is right in front of them. They notice the broken twigs, the sudden silence of birds, the faintest movement in the grass. Humans used to have these same instincts, but modern life has dulled them. The good news is you can sharpen them again with practice.

Start by working on your awareness when you're in public places. Most people walk through life half-asleep, staring at their phones or lost in thought. Try this instead: when you enter a new space, pause for just a second and take in the whole scene. Notice where the exits are. See how people are standing and moving. Pay attention to hands and eyes - these often show what someone is about to do before they do it. You're not looking for danger specifically, just practicing the habit of really seeing what's around you. At first, it might feel awkward or tiring, but after a while, it becomes automatic. Police officers and military personnel train this way because it works - not to make them fearful, but to keep them alert.

There's a concept called "baseline awareness" that helps with this. Every environment has a normal rhythm - how people typically move and sound in a coffee shop versus a subway station versus a park at night. When something breaks that rhythm, that's when you want to take notice. Maybe it's someone moving against the crowd for no clear reason, or a sound that doesn't fit the place you're in.

These don't always mean danger, but they're worth paying attention to. The more you practice recognizing the baseline, the quicker you'll spot when something's off. This isn't about judging people - it's about observing patterns. Most violent situations don't just happen suddenly; there are usually small signs beforehand if you know how to look.

Your peripheral vision is more important than you might think. In dangerous situations, things often come at you from the sides, not straight ahead. You can train your peripheral vision by doing simple exercises. Try sitting in a busy place and keeping your eyes fixed straight ahead while noticing how much you can see to the sides without moving your head. With practice, you'll be able to pick up on movements and details that would have been invisible before. This kind of wide-angle awareness was crucial for ancient warriors who had to watch for attacks from any direction, and it's just as useful today.

Another key skill is learning to trust that feeling when something seems wrong even if you can't say exactly why. That gut reaction comes from your brain picking up on small clues that haven't yet reached your conscious mind. Maybe it's the way someone's standing just a little too still, or how their eyes keep scanning the room in a certain pattern. Whatever it is, that warning feeling exists for a reason. The mistake most people make is talking themselves out of listening to it. They think "I'm probably overreacting" or "I don't want to look paranoid." But paying attention to that feeling doesn't mean you have to act dramatically - it just means you should position yourself a little differently, maybe move closer to an exit or put yourself near other people. Small adjustments can make all the difference.

Light and shadow play a big role in how we see potential threats. In low light, our eyes work differently, and so do the eyes of anyone who might mean us harm. Practice moving through different lighting conditions and notice how your vision changes. Become aware of dark corners and blind spots where someone could be waiting unseen. This doesn't mean avoiding all shadows - that's impossible - but knowing how to use them to your advantage. If you're out at night, try to stay where your eyes have time to adjust to the darkness rather than walking straight from bright light into dark areas. And remember that if you can't see well in a space, neither can anyone else - sometimes just changing your position slightly can give you the visual advantage.

Sound is just as important as sight when it comes to early warning. Train yourself to really listen to your environment, not just the sounds you expect to hear. Most of us tune out background noise completely, but those sounds contain information. The sudden absence of sound can be just as telling as a new noise. Maybe the chatter in a restaurant drops for no obvious reason, or the usual street sounds go quiet. These shifts in the soundscape often happen before visible signs of trouble appear. You don't need to analyze every sound - just stay open to noticing when the normal sounds change in ways that don't make sense.

The best way to develop these skills is to make observation a daily habit, not something you only think about in scary situations. Make a game of noticing details when you're waiting in line or sitting in a park. Try to remember specific things about people who walk by - what they're wearing, how they move, small habits they have. The more you practice this in normal situations, the better it will serve you when it really matters.

These aren't spy techniques or superhuman abilities - they're just ways of paying attention that anyone can learn. Ancient warriors and hunters depended on these skills for survival, and while most of us don't face those kinds of dangers today, the same principles still apply. The world gives us information all the time if we're willing to see it. The key is to look without staring, notice without obsessing, and stay aware without becoming fearful. That balance is what keeps you safe while still letting you live your life.

Remember that this kind of awareness shouldn't make you tense or anxious. It's actually the opposite - the more you practice, the more relaxed you'll feel in your surroundings because you'll know you can trust yourself to notice what's important. Start small, be patient with yourself, and keep at it. Over time, you'll find yourself seeing things others miss and sensing potential problems earlier. That extra second or two of warning can make all the difference when it counts. The goal isn't to see the future - just to see the present more clearly. And that's something anyone can learn to do.

Chapter 4
No Thoughts, Just Action

There comes a moment in every dangerous situation where thinking becomes your worst enemy. That split-second when you pause to consider your options is the same moment you lose your advantage. The people who survive violent encounters aren't necessarily the strongest or fastest - they're the ones who act without hesitation. This might sound simple, but it's one of the hardest things to train because everything in our modern lives teaches us to stop and think first. From childhood we're told to consider consequences, weigh options, be careful. Those are good rules for everyday life, but they'll get you hurt in a real fight. The secret isn't to become thoughtless, but to move your thinking from the moment of action to the time before and after. You prepare your responses in advance so when the time comes, your body knows what to do without waiting for instructions from your brain.

This is why martial arts masters spend countless hours repeating basic movements until they become automatic. They're not just building muscle memory - they're training their nervous system to bypass the thinking process entirely. When a boxer throws a punch in a match, they aren't deciding to punch in that moment. The decision was made long before, in training, and now the body simply executes. You can develop this same kind of instant response for self-defense situations. Start with simple drills like practicing how you would react if someone suddenly grabbed you. Don't overcomplicate it - choose one or two reliable techniques and repeat them until you don't have to think about the steps anymore. The goal is to reach a point where if someone pushes you, your body reacts correctly before you've even registered what happened.

Adrenaline changes how your brain works, and this is why overthinking fails when you need it most. Under extreme stress, fine motor skills deteriorate and complex thought processes slow down. This is why soldiers are trained to rely on simple, repeatable actions rather than complicated plans. A firearm drill might involve hundreds of repetitions of loading and unloading until the hands can do it without the brain's full attention. The same principle applies to hand-to-hand defense. If your response requires multiple precise steps, it will fail when adrenaline hits. But if it's based on gross motor movements you've practiced until they're second nature, you'll still be able to perform even when scared. This is why palm strikes tend to work better than fist strikes for most people in real fights - when hands shake from adrenaline, an open hand is more reliable than a precise punch.

The mental state you're aiming for is often called "empty mind" in martial traditions. It doesn't mean being blank or unaware - it means being free from internal chatter and hesitation. You see this in athletes during peak performance moments. A basketball player taking a free throw isn't thinking about elbow position or follow-through - they've moved past that stage. Their body knows what to do, and thinking would only interfere. This state doesn't happen by accident. It comes from so much practice that the correct action feels more natural than hesitation. For self-defense purposes, you want to reach this point with a few basic protective responses. How you move when someone swings at you, how you create distance when threatened, how you position yourself in a confined space - these should all be trained to the point of automaticity.

One effective training method is to introduce controlled stress while practicing. If you only drill techniques in a calm, safe environment, they'll abandon you when real stress hits. But if you practice while tired, or with loud distractions, or with someone actually coming at you (in a controlled way), you build the ability to perform under pressure. Police and military trainers use exercises like this because they know that skills must be stress-tested to be reliable. You can create simple versions of this yourself. Have a training partner approach you unexpectedly while you're doing something else, or practice your moves right after intense exercise when your heart is racing. The more you associate the correct responses with physical stress, the more likely they are to surface when you need them.

There's an important balance here between automatic response and situational awareness. Acting without thought doesn't mean acting without judgment. The time for assessing a situation is before and after the moment of action, not during. This is why awareness skills are so important - they help you avoid needing to react in the first place. And when action is required, the simpler your response, the more likely it is to work under stress. Complex solutions fail when you're scared. Simple, practiced movements succeed. This is why most traditional martial arts begin with basic forms and stances - they're building the foundation for action without thought.

The modern world doesn't prepare us for this way of operating. We're used to having time to consider, to deliberate, to change our minds. But survival situations don't work that way. When a car skids on ice, you don't have time to think through physics - you either react correctly or you crash. The same applies to physical threats. This doesn't mean being reckless or violent. It means having trained responses ready so you don't freeze when action is required.

The best fighters aren't those who think fastest in the moment - they're those who've moved the thinking to their training time so the moment itself requires no thought at all.

Start small. Pick one basic defensive movement and practice it daily until it feels completely natural. Then add variations - practice it from different positions, with your eyes closed, when startled. The goal isn't to collect dozens of techniques, but to master a few that will serve you when there's no time to think. Over time, you'll find your body beginning to move on its own when needed. That's when you know you're developing true survival instinct. It's not magic - it's the result of consistent, deliberate practice. And it's available to anyone willing to put in the work. The peace of mind that comes from knowing you can trust your body to react correctly is worth every minute of training. In the end, that's what this is all about - not living in fear, but having the quiet confidence that comes from being prepared.

Chapter 5
Fear Is Your Friend

Fear gets a bad reputation. Most people see it as weakness, something to avoid or overcome. But what if you've been looking at fear all wrong? Fear isn't your enemy–it's your oldest survival tool, hardwired into your body over millions of years of evolution. The problem isn't fear itself, but how we respond to it. Ancient warriors knew this secret: fear keeps you alive if you know how to use it. That pounding heart? It's sending extra oxygen to your muscles. Those shaking hands? They're preparing for action. That tunnel vision? It's focusing your mind on the threat. These are gifts, not curses. The difference between someone who freezes and someone who acts comes down to one thing—whether they see fear as fuel or as failure.

Think about how animals use fear in the wild. A deer that senses a predator doesn't waste time debating whether to run—it's already moving. The fear triggers instant action without thought or hesitation. Humans have this same capacity, but we've buried it under layers of overthinking and social conditioning. We've been taught that being afraid means we're weak, so we try to ignore it or push through it. But real strength comes from working with fear, not against it. When you feel fear rising, that's not the time to fight it—that's the time to channel it. Your body is giving you energy; your job is to direct that energy where it needs to go.

Adrenaline is fear's physical manifestation, and understanding how it works changes everything. When you get scared, your body releases a mix of chemicals designed to help you survive. Your pupils dilate to let in more light. Your blood thickens to prevent excessive bleeding from wounds. Your pain tolerance increases. These are superhuman abilities available to you right now—no training required. The challenge is that most people don't know how to handle this surge. They either panic or try to suppress it. Both approaches waste the gift fear is trying to give you. The better way is to acknowledge the fear, feel it fully, then put it to work. This takes practice, but it's simpler than you might think.

Start by reframing how you think about physical fear responses. That dry mouth before a confrontation? It's your body conserving fluids in case of injury. The urge to urinate? It's lightening your load for faster movement. These aren't signs you're inadequate—they're proof your survival systems work perfectly. The key is recognizing these sensations as preparation rather than panic. When you feel them coming on, take a deep breath and think "good—my body is getting ready." This small mental shift prevents the downward spiral where fear of fear makes everything worse.

There's a technique used by emergency responders and soldiers to manage fear in high-stress situations. They call it "tactical breathing," but it's really just controlled exhales that keep you grounded. When fear hits, your natural tendency is to hold your breath or breathe rapidly. Instead, force yourself to exhale completely, then let the inhale happen naturally. This simple act prevents the oxygen overload that leads to dizziness and panic. It also gives you something physical to focus on besides the fear itself. Try it next time you're nervous—exhale fully before speaking or acting. You'll find your mind clears and your body responds better.

Fear also heightens your senses in ways that can work for you if you know how to interpret them. Time really does seem to slow down in dangerous situations—not because the world changes, but because your brain starts processing information faster. This is why people remember traumatic events in such detail. That expanded awareness is there to help you, not overwhelm you. The trick is to focus it productively. Instead of letting your heightened senses make everything seem important, consciously direct your attention to specific useful details–the attacker's stance, available exits, objects that could help you. Fear gives you laser focus; you just need to aim it.

Training with fear is different than training without it. This is why martial arts sparring feels nothing like practicing forms alone, and why fire drills with actual alarms work better than quiet walkthroughs. If you want to perform under pressure, you need to practice under pressure. Create safe but stressful training scenarios where your fear responses activate. Have a friend surprise you with mock attacks at random times. Practice techniques while exhausted. Simulate the chaos of real encounters with loud noises and unpredictable movements. The goal isn't to eliminate fear, but to become comfortable operating with it. Over time, you'll learn to ride the wave of adrenaline instead of being crushed by it.

The stories we tell ourselves about fear matter more than we realize. If you believe fear means you're inadequate, it will paralyze you. If you understand it as your body's way of helping you survive, it becomes an asset. This isn't positive thinking–it's practical biology. Your fear response evolved because it worked. Countless ancestors survived because their fear made them faster, stronger, and more alert. That same capability is in you right now. The difference between freezing and acting often comes down to whether you see the physical sensations as friends or enemies.

Consider how fear manifests differently in everyone. Some people get hot when scared, others feel cold. Some become talkative, others go silent. There's no "right" way to experience fear–only your way. Learn your personal fear responses through safe but challenging experiences. Notice how your body reacts, what thoughts come up, how your perception changes. The more familiar you are with your unique fear signature, the less it will control you. This self-knowledge is more valuable than any fighting technique because it works in every situation, not just physical confrontations.

Fear also teaches you about your real limits–which are almost always beyond what you imagine. Most people quit at the first sign of discomfort, never discovering what they're truly capable of. Training with fear shows you that you can function—even excel—while afraid. This realization changes everything. When you know from experience that fear doesn't have to stop you, it loses its power over your decisions. You stop avoiding challenging situations because you're not afraid of being afraid anymore. This is true courage—not the absence of fear, but the knowledge that you can act despite it.

The final lesson fear teaches is about recovery. After the threat passes, your body needs time to return to normal. This is why people shake after narrow escapes or cry after emergencies–it's the body's way of releasing leftover tension. Don't judge these reactions or try to suppress them. Let them happen. The faster you allow the aftereffects of fear to move through you, the quicker you regain full control. Fighting the recovery process just prolongs it. This is why experienced fighters can go from intense combat to calm conversation so quickly–they've learned to let the fear come and go like weather, without clinging to it or resisting it.

Fear isn't something to conquer or eliminate. It's a tool, a teacher, and an ally. The warrior's edge doesn't come from lacking fear, but from understanding it so completely that every tremor and pulse becomes useful information. When you stop wasting energy fighting your own survival mechanisms, you free up immense reserves of power. This is the secret those ancient masters knew —that fear properly channeled becomes focus, that adrenaline properly directed becomes strength, that the pounding heart isn't a countdown to failure but the drumbeat of readiness. Your fear was never the problem. Your relationship with it was. Change that, and you change everything.

Chapter 6
The Body Remembers

Your muscles have a kind of wisdom that your conscious mind can't match. Think about the last time you caught a falling object without thinking - your hand moved before you realized what was happening. That's your body's memory at work, operating faster than thought. This physical intelligence is what saves lives in dangerous situations, when there's no time to decide what to do. Martial artists have known for centuries that the key to instant reaction isn't faster thinking, but deeper training - the kind that sinks below the level of conscious control. When your body knows what to do on its own, you don't need to rely on quick thinking under pressure. This is why repetition matters more than complexity in real self-defense. Simple movements drilled hundreds of times will serve you better than fancy techniques you've only practiced occasionally.

The process works because of how your nervous system learns. Every time you repeat a movement, you're strengthening specific neural pathways, making that action easier to perform automatically. It's like wearing a path through tall grass - the more you walk it, the clearer and easier it becomes. This is why traditional martial arts use forms or katas - they're not just rituals, but methods for engraving movements into the body's memory. The student who practices a block thousands of times isn't just learning to block - they're teaching their nervous system to recognize when a block is needed and execute it without conscious command. This explains why experienced fighters seem to anticipate attacks - their bodies recognize patterns before their minds have processed them.

Stress affects this body memory in important ways. When adrenaline floods your system, complex motor skills deteriorate while gross motor skills become enhanced. This is why fine movements like small joint manipulations often fail in real fights, while large powerful strikes remain effective. The smart approach is to train movements that will hold up under stress - palm strikes instead of precise punches, simple foot sweeps instead of complex throws. These don't require the same level of fine control when your hands might be shaking and your vision narrowing. The body remembers best what it practices under conditions similar to real use. This is why effective training includes elements of stress - elevated heart rate, distractions, unpredictability. The closer practice matches reality, the more reliable the body's memory will be when needed.

There's an interesting phenomenon where the body sometimes reacts before the brain perceives danger. Have you ever jerked your hand back from something hot before feeling the burn? That's your spinal cord making a survival decision without waiting for your brain. This kind of reflex can be trained for self-defense purposes through specific drills that create automatic responses to common threats. For example, practicing how you'd react if someone suddenly grabs your wrist - after enough repetitions, your body will start to respond correctly before you've consciously registered the attack. This isn't psychic ability - it's your nervous system recognizing patterns and acting on them at lightning speed. The more you train realistic scenarios, the more of these automatic responses you develop.

Sleep plays a surprising role in how the body remembers physical skills. Studies show that people who practice a movement and then sleep perform better the next day than those who stay awake between practice sessions. During sleep, your brain consolidates and reinforces what you've learned physically. This means that spacing out training sessions with good sleep in between can be more effective than cramming all your practice into one long session. It also suggests why consistent, regular training beats occasional intense workouts - the sleep between sessions is when much of the learning actually happens. Those ancient masters who insisted on daily practice weren't just being strict - they were following what we now know about how the nervous system encodes movement memory.

Emotion intensifies physical memory, which explains why

traumatic events create such strong bodily memories. This same principle can work for training - attaching strong positive emotions to practice sessions makes the lessons stick better. This doesn't mean you need dramatic experiences - just bringing full attention and enjoyment to your training helps. The opposite is also true - practicing while distracted or disinterested leads to weaker retention. This is why traditional martial arts often emphasize mindfulness during practice - being fully present creates stronger neural pathways. The body remembers not just the movements, but the state of mind they were learned in. Training with focus and intention pays off when you need those skills under pressure.

Age affects body memory in ways that might surprise you. While young people generally learn new physical skills faster, older practitioners often perform better under stress. This appears to be because well-practiced movements become more deeply encoded over time, more resistant to disruption under pressure. There's a reason many traditional masters peak in their 40s or 50s - their techniques have become so ingrained that nothing shakes them. This is good news for anyone who thinks they're "too old" to start training - while you might learn slower than a teenager, what you do learn may stick better and serve you more reliably. The key is consistent practice over years, not raw speed of initial learning.

Pain creates powerful body memories, which can be both useful and problematic. On one hand, remembering what caused pain helps avoid future injury - this is survival's most basic lesson. But pain memories can also create flinches and hesitations that interfere with effective response. Smart training gradually exposes practitioners to controlled discomfort - learning to take hits without overreacting, working through fatigue without giving up. This builds resilience while preventing the kind of traumatic associations that lead to freezing up. The goal isn't to become indifferent to pain, but to develop the ability to act despite it when necessary. This balanced approach creates body memories that protect without paralyzing.

The environment where you practice matters more than most people realize. Your body remembers not just movements, but the contexts in which they were learned. This is why it's valuable to train in different locations - outdoors, in tight spaces, on uneven ground. The more varied your practice environments, the more adaptable your skills become. If you've only ever practiced in a clean, spacious dojo, your body may struggle to apply those skills in a cluttered bar or dark alley. Traditional martial artists often trained in all weathers and terrains for this reason - they wanted their skills to be accessible anywhere, not just under ideal conditions. Your training space doesn't need to be fancy - it needs to prepare you for real world unpredictability.

Equipment and clothing choices also influence how the body remembers. Practicing always in loose martial arts uniforms may mean your skills don't translate well to everyday clothes. Training occasionally in regular street clothes - including shoes - helps ensure your movements remain practical. Similarly, if you practice self-defense, try it while carrying a bag or wearing a jacket. These small variations prevent your skills from becoming dependent on specific conditions. The body remembers what you actually practice, not what you intend it to remember. Smart training anticipates the realities of when and how skills might be needed.

Rhythm and flow play important roles in physical memory. Movements connected in smooth sequences are easier to recall than isolated techniques. This is why martial arts forms exist - they link techniques together in memorable patterns. Even if you don't practice traditional forms, creating your own short combinations can help cement skills. The rhythm provides a kind of physical mnemonics, where one movement naturally cues the next. This explains why flowing drills often feel more satisfying and stick better than static repetition - our bodies are wired to remember stories and patterns better than disconnected facts. Building this connectivity into your practice makes techniques more accessible under stress.

The way you breathe during practice becomes part of your body's memory too. Many people hold their breath when performing difficult movements, but this habit will fail them under stress. Consciously practicing with proper breathing - exhaling on exertion, maintaining steady rhythm - ensures your body remembers to breathe when it matters most. This is especially crucial for high-intensity situations where oxygen management makes the difference between lasting and gassing out. Your body will remember what you train it to do, so train with the breathing patterns you'll need in real application.

Ultimately, the body remembers what you give it to remember through consistent, mindful practice. There are no shortcuts to reliable instinctive response - just the steady accumulation of quality repetitions. But the payoff is immense: the ability to act correctly before thought kicks in, to move with certainty when it matters most. This physical wisdom doesn't replace conscious training - it's the fruit of it. Every good repetition is a deposit in your body's memory bank, there for you when you need to make a sudden withdrawal. Start small, be patient, and trust the process. Your body wants to remember - you just need to give it something worth remembering.

Chapter 7
The Invisible Shield

There's something beyond the physical techniques in martial arts that often gets overlooked–the ability to sense trouble before it happens. You might call it intuition, gut feeling, or a sixth sense, but whatever name you give it, this awareness acts like an invisible shield. It's not magic or some mystical power–it's your brain picking up on subtle clues and patterns without your conscious mind realizing it. Think about times you've walked into a room and immediately felt something was off, even if you couldn't point to why. Or moments when you've met someone new and instantly knew not to trust them, despite them saying all the right things. That's your built-in warning system at work, and like any skill, it can be sharpened with practice.

The first step in developing this shield is learning to pay attention to those subtle feelings instead of dismissing them. Most of us have been taught to ignore our instincts in favor of being polite or not wanting to overreact. But those gut feelings exist for a reason–your subconscious mind processes thousands of details your conscious mind misses. Maybe it's the way someone's eyes dart around too much when they talk, or how a supposedly empty parking lot feels strangely quiet. These small signals add up to create that uneasy feeling you can't quite explain. The people who get caught off guard are usually the ones who talked themselves out of listening to that internal alarm. Start by noticing when you get these feelings and what might have triggered them. Over time, you'll start recognizing the patterns your subconscious already knows.

Your body often knows danger before your brain does. That sudden chill down your spine or the hairs standing up on your arms aren't just random reactions—they're physiological responses to potential threats. Ancient warriors paid close attention to these bodily signals because they understood their survival value. In modern times, we've learned to ignore these sensations, writing them off as nerves or imagination. But your body's warning system has been refined over millions of years of evolution—it's worth taking seriously. Next time you feel that unexplained tension or unease, don't brush it aside. Pause for a moment and scan your environment with all your senses. Look for exits, note people's positions, check for anything that seems out of place. This isn't paranoia—it's simply acknowledging that your body might be picking up on something your conscious mind hasn't registered yet.

Your peripheral vision holds more power than you might realize when it comes to sensing danger. While your central vision is great for focusing on details, your peripheral vision detects movement and anomalies much faster. This is why you can sense someone approaching from the side even when you're looking straight ahead. You can train this ability by practicing "soft focus"–keeping your gaze relaxed and wide rather than locked intensely on one spot. Try sitting in a public place and letting your vision expand to take in the whole scene without focusing on any particular person or object. Notice how much movement and activity you can detect without looking directly at it. This expanded awareness gives you more information about your environment and helps you spot potential threats earlier.

Sound provides another layer of your invisible shield. Most people go through life tuning out background noise, but those sounds contain valuable information about your surroundings. The sudden absence of sound can be just as telling as an unexpected noise. Maybe the usual chatter in a restaurant drops for no apparent reason, or street noises go quiet at an odd time. These shifts often happen right before visible trouble appears. You don't need to analyze every sound–just stay open to noticing when the normal soundscape changes in ways that don't make sense. Try this exercise: close your eyes for a minute wherever you are and just listen. Identify how many distinct sounds you can hear and where they're coming from. Regular practice of this simple exercise will sharpen your auditory awareness significantly.

How you carry yourself affects whether you become a target in the first place. Predators–whether animal or human–look for signs of vulnerability. Your posture, gait, and general presence broadcast signals you might not realize. Walking with slumped shoulders and downcast eyes sends a very different message than moving with relaxed awareness. This doesn't mean adopting some tough-guy swagger–that often looks insecure and try-hard. Natural confidence and ease make you a less appealing target because they suggest you'd be more trouble than you're worth. Practice moving through the world with quiet assurance–head up but not stiff, shoulders relaxed, movements smooth and purposeful. This kind of presence creates an invisible barrier that often prevents trouble before it starts.

Your environment constantly provides information if you know how to read it. Reflections in windows let you see behind you without turning your head. Changes in lighting can reveal movement around corners. The behavior of animals and birds often signals approaching people before you see them. These observational skills were second nature to our ancestors but have atrophied in modern life. You can reawaken them simply by paying more attention as you go about your day. Make a game of noticing details—how many people are in the room behind you right now without looking? What color was the last car that passed by? Who entered or left the space you're in recently? This isn't about being constantly vigilant to the point of exhaustion—it's about engaging more fully with your surroundings instead of moving through the world on autopilot.

Breathing plays an unexpected role in your awareness shield. When people get nervous or sense danger, they often hold their breath or breathe shallowly without realizing it.

This actually reduces your awareness and reaction speed because your brain isn't getting enough oxygen. Consciously maintaining steady, deep breaths keeps your senses sharp and your mind clear. Try this: when you enter a new environment or feel that first twinge of unease, take three slow, deep breaths while scanning your surroundings. This simple act does two important things–it oxygenates your brain for better thinking, and it gives you a moment to assess before reacting. That brief pause can mean the difference between a smart response and a panicked one.

Trust plays a complicated role in personal safety. While it's nice to believe the best about people, your invisible shield works best when combined with reasonable caution. This doesn't mean assuming everyone means you harm—that would be exhausting and unnecessary. It does mean maintaining awareness until people have earned your trust rather than giving it automatically. Notice how someone behaves, not just what they say. Pay attention to whether their words match their actions. See how they treat others when they think no one important is watching. These observations give you much better information than first impressions or smooth talk. The ability to accurately assess people is perhaps the most powerful part of your invisible shield.

Technology has changed how we need to use our awareness. Staring at phones in public places makes people easy targets because it removes their primary defense–attention. If you must use your phone in transit or in crowded areas, practice doing so while maintaining some environmental awareness. Keep one earbud out so you can still hear surroundings. Glance up frequently to scan your environment. Position yourself so no one can approach unseen from behind. These small adjustments let you stay connected without becoming vulnerable. Remember that no text message is so urgent it's worth getting mugged over—if a situation feels sketchy, put the phone away and focus on getting to safety.

Your invisible shield works best when it's maintained without constant conscious effort. Like any skill, it becomes stronger and more automatic with regular practice. Start small—maybe spend just ten minutes a day being extra observant during your commute or lunch break. Notice people's body language, watch for unusual patterns in your environment, check in with your gut feelings about situations. Over time, these habits will become second nature, giving you that subtle edge in sensing and avoiding trouble. The goal isn't to live in fear–it's to move through the world with relaxed awareness that lets you enjoy life while staying safe. That's the real power of the invisible shield–it protects without imprisoning, warns without paralyzing, and gives you the freedom that comes with true confidence in your ability to handle whatever comes your way.

Chapter 8
One Move, One Kill

The most effective fighters throughout history didn't rely on complicated techniques or flashy moves–they mastered a few simple actions that worked when it mattered most. There's a saying in martial arts that it's better to know one move you've practiced ten thousand times than ten thousand moves you've practiced once. This chapter is about finding those few reliable techniques that will serve you in real situations, not demonstrations or competitions. When adrenaline is pumping and seconds count, complexity fails. What works is simple, direct, and brutally efficient movement that doesn't require perfect conditions to be effective. The goal isn't to impress anyone with your skill—it's to survive and walk away unharmed.

Start by identifying your natural weapons—the parts of your body that can deliver powerful strikes without much training. Your elbows and knees are excellent examples; they're hard, difficult to injure when used properly, and generate tremendous force even without perfect form. An elbow strike to the jaw or a knee to the thigh can disable an attacker much more reliably than a fancy spinning kick that requires distance, timing, and balance to execute. Your palms are another underrated weapon—a heel-palm strike to the nose or chin is devastatingly effective and much safer for your hands than closed-fist punches. These basic strikes work because they use your body's natural structure rather than requiring precise alignment or years of training to master.

Footwork might not seem exciting, but it's more important than any striking technique. Being able to move quickly and maintain balance is what allows you to attack effectively or escape when needed. Simple steps that get you out of the line of attack while keeping you balanced require far less practice than elaborate dodges or rolls. Practice moving from your center–not just with your legs, but by shifting your whole body weight smoothly. This kind of movement should feel natural, like catching yourself when you slip on ice–your body already knows how to do it, you just need to refine that instinct. Good footwork lets you control distance, which determines whether you can strike effectively or need to escape. The fighter who controls the distance controls the fight.

Clinch fighting is another area where simplicity wins. When distance closes and you're grappling with an attacker, complicated submissions and counters often fail under stress. What works are basic principles–maintaining good posture, controlling the opponent's head, and using your whole body rather than just arm strength. A simple headlock escape, for instance, works better when you understand the principle of moving your whole body to create space rather than just trying to pull away with your arms. These fundamentals apply across various situations, making them more valuable than specific techniques that only work in ideal circumstances. The time to learn how to handle close quarters isn't when someone's trying to tackle you—it's in calm, controlled practice sessions where you can ingrain the right movements.

Defensive skills matter more than offensive ones for most people. Blocking might not seem as exciting as striking, but preventing damage is more important than delivering it in a survival situation. The good news is that basic defensive movements are easier to learn than most offensive techniques. A high guard to protect your head, checking kicks with your shin, and basic parries can be learned quickly and refined over time. These defenses should become automatic through repetition so they work even when you're surprised or scared. It's far better to reliably block most attacks than to occasionally land spectacular counters that leave you open the rest of the time.

The mental approach to techniques is just as important as the physical execution. Many traditional martial arts emphasize the concept of "one strike, one kill"–not literally killing with every blow, but the mindset that each movement should be decisive and committed. Half-hearted techniques waste energy and often fail when you need them most. This doesn't mean you should always use maximum force–it means whatever level of force you choose should be delivered with complete commitment. A firm push to create space requires the same mental focus as a powerful strike–the difference is in degree, not in quality. This mindset develops through practice where you treat every repetition seriously, not just going through the motions.

Training for reality means preparing for imperfect situations. Most attacks happen unexpectedly, often when you're not in an ideal stance or ready position. This is why it's valuable to practice your techniques from awkward positions–getting up from a chair, while turning around, or when caught off-balance. These variations build adaptability that serves you better than perfect form under perfect conditions. If your techniques only work when you're perfectly balanced and prepared, they'll fail when you need them most. The best techniques are those that work even when executed poorly–because in real situations, perfect execution is rare.

Weapons can be part of this simple approach, but with an important caveat–the best weapon is one you're likely to have with you when needed. Fancy combat knives or tactical tools are useless if they're sitting in a drawer at home. Everyday objects–pens, keys, a heavy book–can become effective weapons if you understand basic principles of striking and targeting. The same simplicity applies here–thrusting with a pen toward vulnerable targets like the eyes or throat requires less precision than complicated disarms or fancy knife techniques. The key is recognizing what's available in your environment and how it can create distance or create an opening to escape.

Recovery after executing a technique is just as important as the technique itself. Many people practice strikes or blocks but neglect what comes next–regaining balance, checking for additional threats, and positioning for either continued defense or escape. This transition moment is where many fights are won or lost. A good technique followed by hesitation or poor positioning can undo all the advantage you gained. Practice always includes the before, during, and after of each movement–not just the technique in isolation. This complete approach builds habits that serve you in fluid, unpredictable situations.

The test of any technique is whether it works when you're tired, scared, and surprised. This is why conditioning matters–both physical conditioning to have the stamina to keep fighting, and mental conditioning to keep functioning under stress. Techniques that require perfect timing or enormous strength often fail when you're exhausted. Those based on body mechanics and simple principles keep working even when you're not at your best. This reliability under adverse conditions is what makes certain techniques stand the test of time across various martial arts and combat systems.

Ultimately, having a few simple, reliable techniques that you've practiced until they're second nature is far more valuable than knowing hundreds of moves you can't execute under pressure. The martial artist who can remain calm and execute their basics perfectly in chaos will defeat the one with extensive knowledge but no reliable tools. This philosophy extends beyond physical techniques–it's about identifying what works and focusing your training there rather than constantly chasing new information. Depth beats breadth when your life might depend on it. Find those few moves that feel natural and effective for you, drill them relentlessly under increasingly challenging conditions, and trust that when the moment comes, your body will know what to do. That's the real meaning of "one move, one kill"–not literal destruction, but the confidence that comes from having a few tools you can wield with absolute certainty.

Chapter 9
Stress Training

The difference between practicing in a safe, controlled environment and facing real danger comes down to how your body reacts under stress. You can know every technique perfectly when you're calm, but if you freeze when adrenaline hits, that knowledge won't help you. This is why stress training matters—it bridges the gap between theory and reality. The goal isn't to eliminate your body's stress response—that's impossible and would actually be dangerous. Instead, you need to learn how to function despite the shaking hands, tunnel vision, and racing heart that come with adrenaline. This kind of training has been used by warriors and fighters for centuries, not because they understood the science behind it, but because they saw what worked when lives were on the line.

Start by understanding what happens to your body under stress. When your brain perceives danger, it triggers a flood of chemicals that prepare you to fight or run. Your heart rate spikes to pump more blood to your muscles. Your pupils dilate to let in more light. Non-essential functions like digestion slow down so energy can go where it's needed most. These changes are helpful for survival, but they interfere with fine motor skills and complex thinking. That's why people under stress often fumble with keys or forget simple things—their body is prioritizing raw strength and speed over precision and careful thought. The secret isn't trying to stop this reaction, but training your skills to work within it.

One effective method is to practice your techniques while physically exhausted. When your muscles are tired and your heart is pounding from exercise, you're already in a state similar to the stress response. Try doing a set of push-ups or sprints until you're breathing hard, then immediately practice your defensive moves or strikes. You'll notice immediately how different it feels compared to practicing when fresh. Your movements might be sloppier, your balance less steady–this is exactly why you need to train this way. Over time, you'll learn to compensate for these changes and maintain effectiveness even when exhausted. Soldiers and athletes have used this approach for generations because it works–skills trained under fatigue hold up when it matters.

Another key element is introducing unpredictability to your training. If you always practice with a partner who attacks in predictable ways from predictable angles, you're not preparing for reality. Have training partners vary their timing, speed, and types of attacks so you never know exactly what's coming. This uncertainty creates mild stress that mimics real encounters far better than scripted drills. You can start simple—maybe have a partner raise their hand randomly during a conversation and see how quickly you can react when they suddenly move toward you. These little surprises train your brain to stay alert and respond to genuine threats rather than practiced patterns.

Adding distractions during training is another way to simulate stress. Real fights don't happen in quiet dojos with perfect lighting–there's noise, movement, chaos. Try practicing your techniques with loud music playing, people moving around you, or flashing lights. This trains your ability to focus despite sensory overload, which is exactly what you need when adrenaline is narrowing your attention. Police and military trainers often use smoke, loud bangs, and other distractions during exercises because they know that skills must work despite chaos, not just in ideal conditions. You don't need fancy equipment to apply this principle–

just introducing some controlled confusion to your practice sessions can make a big difference.

Pain tolerance is another aspect of stress training. This doesn't mean seeking out unnecessary injury, but learning to function despite discomfort. Simple exercises like holding a challenging stance until your muscles burn, or continuing to practice while slightly injured (without making things worse) build mental toughness. The ability to push through pain and keep going can make the difference in survival situations. Many traditional martial arts include conditioning exercises not just to strengthen the body, but to teach students how to perform while uncomfortable. This isn't about being macho–it's practical preparation for times when you might have to fight through pain to survive.

Breathing control becomes even more important under stress. When adrenaline hits, most people either hold their breath or breathe rapidly, which only increases panic and reduces oxygen to the brain. Practice maintaining steady breathing even during intense exercise or surprise drills. One method is to count your breaths during stressful training–in for four counts, hold for four, out for four. This gives your mind something to focus on besides the stress and prevents the oxygen depletion that leads to poor decision-making. Firefighters and emergency responders use similar techniques to stay calm during crises–it's not about eliminating stress, but preventing it from overwhelming your ability to function.

Emotional stress is just as important to train for as physical stress. Many people can handle physical discomfort but freeze when confronted with shouting, threats, or the fear of embarrassment. Include verbal aggression in your training–

have partners yell insults or threats while you practice maintaining focus. This isn't about getting used to abuse, but about learning to stay calm when someone is trying to emotionally overwhelm you. Most violent encounters begin with verbal confrontation, and being able to think clearly during this phase can often prevent physical conflict altogether. The ability to remain composed when someone is screaming in your face is a skill like any other–it can be trained.

After-action recovery is a frequently overlooked part of stress training. How you come down from a stressful event affects your ability to handle the next one. Practice calming techniques immediately after intense training sessions—controlled breathing, shaking out tension, consciously relaxing muscles. This trains your body to return to baseline quickly rather than staying amped up for hours. In real situations, you might need to handle multiple threats or make important decisions shortly after a confrontation. Being able to regain composure quickly is just as valuable as the initial stress response.

Gradual exposure is key to effective stress training. Just as you wouldn't try to lift your maximum weight on the first day at the gym, you shouldn't jump into extreme stress scenarios before building up tolerance. Start with mild stressors–maybe practicing techniques after light exercise–and gradually increase intensity as you adapt. This progressive approach builds resilience without overwhelming your system. Special forces units use this principle in their training pipelines–recruits aren't thrown into the most brutal exercises immediately, but work up to them over time. Sustainable stress training follows the same pattern of gradual challenge and recovery.

The ultimate goal isn't to become immune to stress, but to expand your window of tolerance—the range of stress in which you can still think clearly and act effectively. Everyone has a breaking point, but through proper training, that point moves further and further out. This expanded capacity serves you in all areas of life, not just physical confrontations. Job interviews, public speaking, emergencies—all become more manageable when you've trained your stress response. The ancient warriors who could remain calm amid battle weren't born different—they trained systematically to handle what would overwhelm others.

Remember that stress training isn't about toughness for its own sake. Every exercise should have a clear purpose tied to real-world needs. Ask yourself how each drill translates to potential situations you might face. Urban self-defense requires different stress training than wilderness survival or competitive fighting. Tailor your approach to your actual life and concerns. A parent defending their child needs different stress skills than a soldier in combat–both need training, but the specifics vary.

Consistency matters more than intensity in stress training. Short, regular sessions where you push your comfort zone slightly create lasting adaptation better than occasional extreme challenges. Think of it like building calluses–frequent mild friction creates durable protection better than occasional burns. Ten minutes of daily stress training will serve you better than monthly marathon sessions. This approach also prevents burnout and injury while allowing steady progress.

The true test of stress training comes not in the dojo or gym, but in everyday life. Notice how you handle unexpected challenges, frustrations, and minor crises. These are opportunities to apply the same principles—maintaining focus despite discomfort, controlling your breathing, pushing through difficulty. The warrior's mindset isn't something you turn on and off—it's a way of moving through the world that gets stronger with use. Stress training isn't just preparation for worst-case scenarios—it's practice for living with resilience and presence no matter what comes your way.

What makes this approach different from just toughing things out is the element of awareness. Pay attention to how your body and mind react under different types of stress—what triggers you, what helps you recover, where your breaking points are. This self-knowledge is more valuable than any specific technique because it lets you adapt your training to your unique needs. Two people might need completely different stress training to address their personal challenges. The common thread is the commitment to face those challenges rather than avoid them.

In the end, stress training isn't about becoming fearless–it's about becoming functional despite fear. The warrior who seems calm in danger isn't unafraid; they've simply learned how to act effectively while afraid. This ability doesn't come from any special talent, but from the willingness to regularly step outside comfort and practice performing under pressure. Start where you are, be consistent, and trust the process. The confidence that comes from knowing you can handle stress is worth every difficult moment of training. That confidence isn't loud or showy–it's the quiet certainty of someone who's faced their limits and learned how to move beyond them.

Chapter 10
The Unbreakable Mind

The final piece of the puzzle isn't about physical technique or reaction speed–it's about the mental resilience that keeps you going when everything in you wants to quit. There's a moment in every fight, every crisis, every hard situation where the outcome hinges not on skill, but on sheer stubbornness–the refusal to give up even when it feels hopeless. This quality separates survivors from victims more than any physical attribute. You can have perfect technique, lightning reflexes, and endless stamina, but if your mind breaks under pressure, none of it matters. The unbreakable mind isn't something you're born with–it's built through deliberate practice and conscious choice, one small decision at a time.

Start by understanding that mental toughness isn't about ignoring pain or fear–it's about acknowledging those feelings and continuing anyway. The people who crumble under pressure are often the ones who believe they shouldn't be feeling what they're feeling. They think, "I shouldn't be this scared," or "This shouldn't be so hard," and that thought alone drains their energy. The mentally tough don't waste energy arguing with reality–they accept what is and focus on what to do next. This isn't resignation; it's clarity. When you stop fighting the fact that a situation is difficult, you free up energy to actually deal with it. Next time you're in a challenging training session or facing something hard, try this shift: instead of thinking "this is too hard," think "this is what hard feels like." That simple reframe removes the internal resistance that exhausts people before the real work even begins.

Small daily habits build mental resilience more than occasional heroic efforts. Making yourself get out of bed immediately when the alarm goes off, finishing workouts even when you're tired, sticking to commitments when it's inconvenient—these seemingly insignificant choices strengthen your ability to push through when it really counts. The mind learns from repetition: every time you follow through on something difficult, you reinforce the neural pathways that say "I don't quit." Conversely, every time you take the easy way out, you strengthen the habit of giving up. This is why ancient warrior traditions emphasized discipline in all areas of life—not because they were obsessed with rules, but because they understood that how you do anything is how you do everything. The willpower you cultivate by forcing yourself to train on rainy days is the same willpower that will keep you fighting when exhausted and injured.

Pain is inevitable in hard training and real fights, but suffering is optional. There's a crucial difference between the two–pain is the physical sensation; suffering is the mental story you layer on top of it. When most people feel pain, they immediately start thinking, "This hurts too much, I can't take it, I need to stop." That internal dialogue is what actually breaks people, not the pain itself. Navy SEALs have a saying: "The only easy day was yesterday." It's not just a motivational slogan–it's a mental tool. By expecting and accepting that things will be hard, they remove the mental friction that comes from hoping for comfort. You can apply this same principle in your training. When something hurts, instead of thinking, "This shouldn't be happening," try thinking, "This is what I signed up for." It sounds simple, but this shift removes the extra layer of resistance that turns pain into suffering.

Visualization is another powerful tool for building an unbreakable mind. Athletes and soldiers have used this technique for decades because it works. The idea isn't to fantasize about easy victories, but to mentally rehearse handling difficult situations with composure. Spend a few minutes each day visualizing yourself staying calm and effective under stress— maybe handling an unexpected attack, pushing through exhaustion in training, or dealing with an emergency. Make the scenarios as vivid as possible, engaging all your senses. This mental practice creates neural pathways almost as strong as physical training, so when real challenges come, your brain recognizes them as familiar territory rather than shocking surprises. The key is consistency–five minutes of daily visualization does more than an hour once a month.

Your self-talk under stress matters more than you might realize. In tough moments, most people's inner monologue becomes their worst enemy– "I can't do this," "This is too much," "I'm going to fail." These thoughts become self-fulfilling prophecies. The solution isn't unrealistic positive thinking, but neutral, factual self-talk. Instead of saying, "This is impossible," try, "This is difficult, but I've handled hard things before." Instead of, "I can't take it," try, "I'll do one more minute, then reassess." This kind of internal dialogue keeps you moving forward without denying reality. Special operators often use counting or checklists under stress for this exact reason—it keeps their mind focused on concrete actions rather than spiraling into panic. You can practice this in everyday life by noticing your internal monologue during minor stresses and consciously shifting it toward neutral, action-oriented statements.

Purpose is the ultimate anchor for the unbreakable mind. People can endure incredible hardship when they have a strong enough reason. In survival situations, those who have someone depending on them often outlast those who are alone. This is why clarifying your "why" is so important–when training feels pointless or a fight seems unwinnable, that deeper purpose keeps you going. Your "why" doesn't need to be dramatic–maybe it's protecting your family, honoring your training, or simply refusing to be a victim. Whatever it is, the more clearly you define it beforehand, the more power it will have when you need it. Spend time regularly reflecting on why you train and what you're willing to endure. That clarity becomes a lifeline in hard moments.

Recovery is part of resilience, not opposed to it. The unbreakable mind isn't one that never rests—it's one that knows when to push and when to recover. Overtraining leads to breakdowns just as surely as weakness does. This is why elite athletes schedule rest days and why special forces units build recovery time into hellish training cycles. Pushing through fatigue is important, but so is knowing when to stop and recharge. The difference between toughness and stupidity is awareness—toughness listens to the body's signals and responds appropriately. Apply this to your training by alternating hard days with easier ones, taking time to stretch and recover, and getting enough sleep. Mental resilience requires physical fuel–you can't think clearly when exhausted or malnourished.

Community and shared hardship forge mental toughness in ways solo training can't. There's a reason military units train together rather than alone–shared suffering creates bonds that push people beyond their perceived limits. When you're ready to quit, seeing others continue gives you strength to keep going. This doesn't mean you can't develop resilience alone, but finding even one training partner multiplies your endurance. The accountability of knowing someone expects you to show up, the encouragement of shared struggle, the unwillingness to let them down–these social elements access reserves of willpower that remain untapped in isolation. If possible, find others committed to similar growth and train together regularly. The right group will pull you through when your own motivation falters.

Finally, understand that the unbreakable mind is a practice, not a destination. There's no finish line where you're suddenly immune to doubt or fatigue. Even the most hardened warriors have moments of weakness–what sets them apart is the habit of continuing anyway. Some days your training will feel effortless; other days just showing up will be a victory. Both are part of the process. The measure of your resilience isn't whether you ever struggle, but how quickly you regain footing when knocked down. Like a tree that grows stronger from weathering storms, your mind toughens each time it pushes through difficulty.

This mental strength spills over into every area of life. The discipline to train when tired becomes the discipline to work hard when unmotivated. The courage to face physical challenge becomes the courage to have difficult conversations. The resilience to continue a hard workout becomes the resilience to persevere through life's inevitable setbacks. The warrior's mindset isn't just for fighting–it's for living with intention and grit no matter what comes.

Start small. Next time you want to quit but don't need to, pause for ten seconds before giving in. In those seconds, ask yourself, "Can I do just a little more?" Often, you'll find you can. That's how resilience grows—not through grand gestures, but through countless small decisions to keep going. Over time, these choices add up to an unshakable confidence that no matter what happens, you'll find a way through. That confidence isn't loud or boastful—it's the quiet certainty of someone who's tested their limits and knows what they're capable of. That's the unbreakable mind.

About the Author

Liang Wei Hao is an emerging author whose vivid narratives blend the rich tapestry of Chinese culture with timeless themes of courage and discovery. With a degree in philosophy and a passion for historical folklore, Liang crafts stories that resonate with depth and authenticity. When not writing, he can be found exploring ancient temples, practicing martial arts, or savoring spicy Sichuan noodles. Liang Wei Hao lives in a bustling city, where the hum of urban life fuels his creative spirit, inviting readers to embark on unforgettable journeys through his words.

www.ingramcontent.com/pod-product-compliance
Ingram Content Group UK Ltd.
Pitfield, Milton Keynes, MK11 3LW, UK
UKHW021009131025
8353UKWH00014B/116